# DIGITAL CITIZENSHIP
# STAYING SAFE ONLINE

by Kristine Spanier, MLIS

PASSWORD
PROTECTED

CONFIRM

click here for more information

pogo

# Ideas for Parents and Teachers

Pogo Books let children practice reading informational text while introducing them to nonfiction features such as headings, labels, sidebars, maps, and diagrams, as well as a table of contents, glossary, and index.

Carefully leveled text with a strong photo match offers early fluent readers the support they need to succeed.

## Before Reading

• "Walk" through the book and point out the various nonfiction features. Ask the student what purpose each feature serves.
• Look at the glossary together. Read and discuss the words.

## Read the Book

• Have the child read the book independently.
• Invite him or her to list questions that arise from reading.

## After Reading

• Discuss the child's questions. Talk about how he or she might find answers to those questions.
• Prompt the child to think more. Ask: Has anyone asked you for personal information online? What did you do about it?

Pogo Books are published by Jump!
5357 Penn Avenue South
Minneapolis, MN 55419
www.jumplibrary.com

Library of Congress Cataloging-in-Publication Data

Names: Spanier, Kristine, author.
Title: Staying safe online / by Kristine Spanier, MLIS.
Description: Minneapolis, MN: Jump!, [2019]
Series: Digital citizenship | Includes index.
Identifiers: LCCN 2018037625 (print)
LCCN 2018040116 (ebook)
ISBN 9781641284462 (ebook)
ISBN 9781641284448 (hardcover: alk. paper)
ISBN 9781641284455 (pbk.)
Subjects: LCSH: Internet and children–Juvenile literature. | Online etiquette–Juvenile literature. | Computer crimes–Prevention–Juvenile literature.
Classification: LCC HQ784.I58 (ebook) | LCC HQ784.I58 S658 2019 (print) | DDC 004.67/8083–dc23
LC record available at https://lccn.loc.gov/2018037625

Editor: Jenna Trnka
Designer: Michelle Sonnek

Photo Credits: Africa Studio/Shutterstock, cover; Julian Rovagnati/Shutterstock, 1 (background); Rawpixel.com/Shutterstock, 1 (foreground), 5; Georgejmclittle/Shutterstock, 3; all_about_people/Shutterstock, 4; Daisy Daisy/Shutterstock, 6-7; Y Photo Studio/Shutterstock, 8-9; Anastasiya 99/Shutterstock, 10-11 (background); Panimoni/Shutterstock, 10-11 (foreground); ferlistockphoto/iStock, 12; Syda Productions/Shutterstock, 13; Evgeny Karandaev/Shutterstock, 14-15 (background); marysuperstudio/Shutterstock, 14-15 (foreground); GUNDAM_Ai/Shutterstock, 16-17 (background); Adrian windle/Shutterstock, 16-17 (foreground); NIKS ADS/Shutterstock, 18; wavebreakmedia/Shutterstock, 19; Kinga/Shutterstock, 20-21; 131pixfoto/Shutterstock, 23.

Printed in the United States of America at Corporate Graphics in North Mankato, Minnesota.

# TABLE OF CONTENTS

# CHAPTER 1

. . . . . . . . . . . . . . . . . . . . . . . . . . . . . . . . . . . . . . . .

# ONLINE RISKS

We are online nearly every day. Why? To play games. Do homework. Shop. Find information. Chat with friends.

More than three billion people are online with us! Most are online for the same reasons we are. But some people want to cause harm.

**Cyberbullies** are online to make people feel bad. This is wrong. What can you do to stop them? Don't reply to their comments. Block them from your device. Tell an adult.

Some adults pretend they are children online. They may seem friendly. How? They play the same games you do. They make nice comments. They build your trust.

Then they might ask for photos. Or ask you to call them. They might ask for your address or the name of your school. They may want to meet you in real life. This is dangerous.

## WHAT DO YOU THINK?

Never share information with people you don't know in real life. Don't call them. Don't send photos. Never agree to meet them. Why do you think this is important?

**Malware** is also dangerous. What is it? Programs created to give computers **viruses**. We are tricked into downloading them. They might appear in **pop-up windows**. Your passwords and other private information are at risk. Never download anything or install **software** without an adult's permission.

## DID YOU KNOW?

Don't give your birth date or email address to someone you don't know. This information is all someone may need to get more **personal information** about you. They may try to get into your bank account. Or get credit cards in your name.

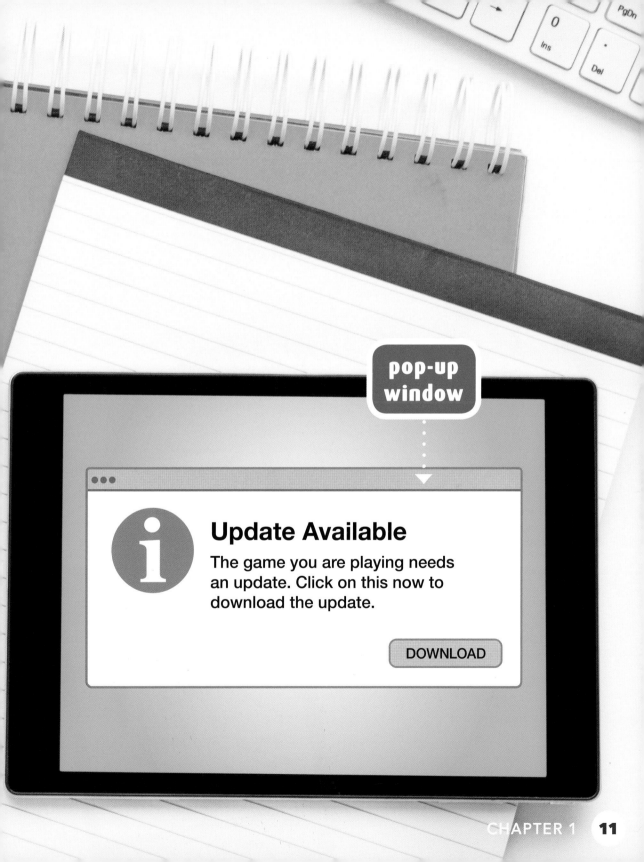

**pop-up window**

# Update Available

The game you are playing needs an update. Click on this now to download the update.

DOWNLOAD

# CHAPTER 2

· · · · · · · · · · · · · · · · · · · · · · · · · · · · · · · · · · · · · · · · · · · · ·

# PROTECT YOUR PRIVACY

Protect your **privacy** online. Do you post photos while on vacation? People who are not your friends may see them. They know you are gone. This can put your home at risk.

Wait until you return to post photos. Better yet, show them to your friends in person.

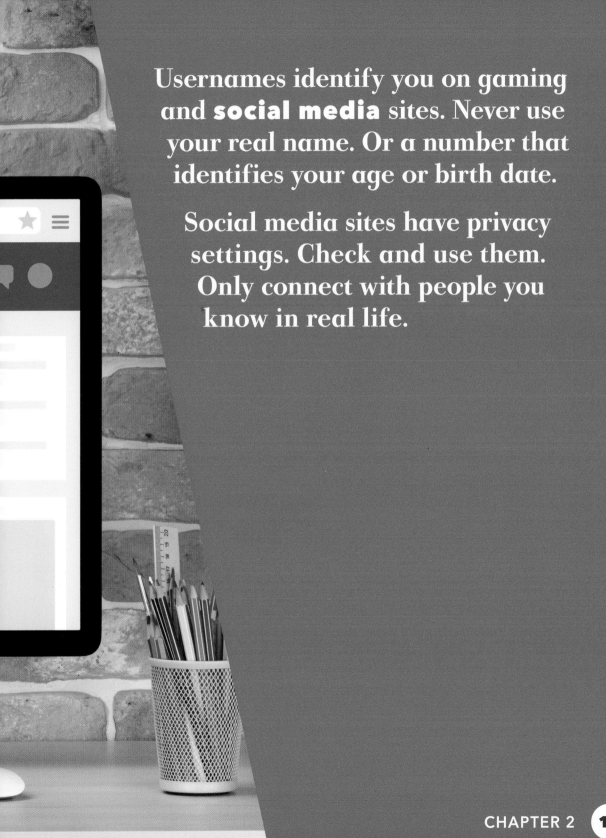

Usernames identify you on gaming and **social media** sites. Never use your real name. Or a number that identifies your age or birth date.

Social media sites have privacy settings. Check and use them. Only connect with people you know in real life.

You might get an email that looks like it is from a real person or company. It could ask for personal information. Or a password to an account. This is called **phishing**. It is a trick. Never reply to these emails. Block them.

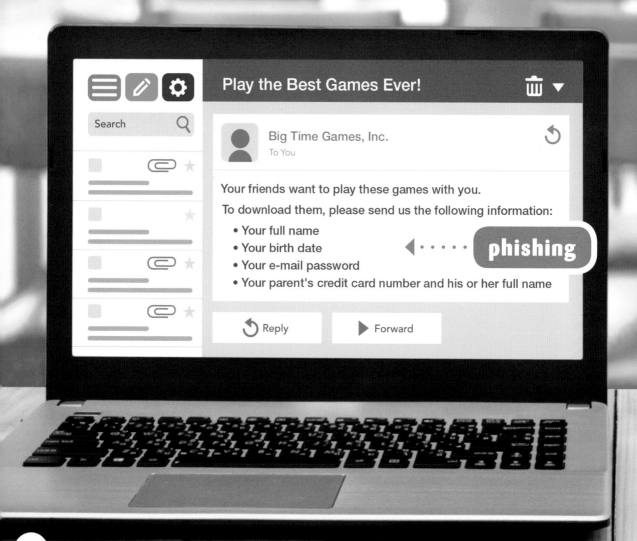

# TAKE A LOOK!

Passwords are private. Only share them with your parents or guardians. What makes a strong password?

- Use a combination of numbers, letters, and symbols.
- Make it 12 characters or longer.
- Don't use your phone number.
- Don't use your birth date.
- Don't use your **Social Security number**.
- Don't use the same password on different sites.

# CHAPTER 3

## DIGITAL CITIZEN

Be a good digital citizen. Only make kind comments. Your words can stay on the Internet for years. Are your friends being cyberbullies? Tell them to stop.

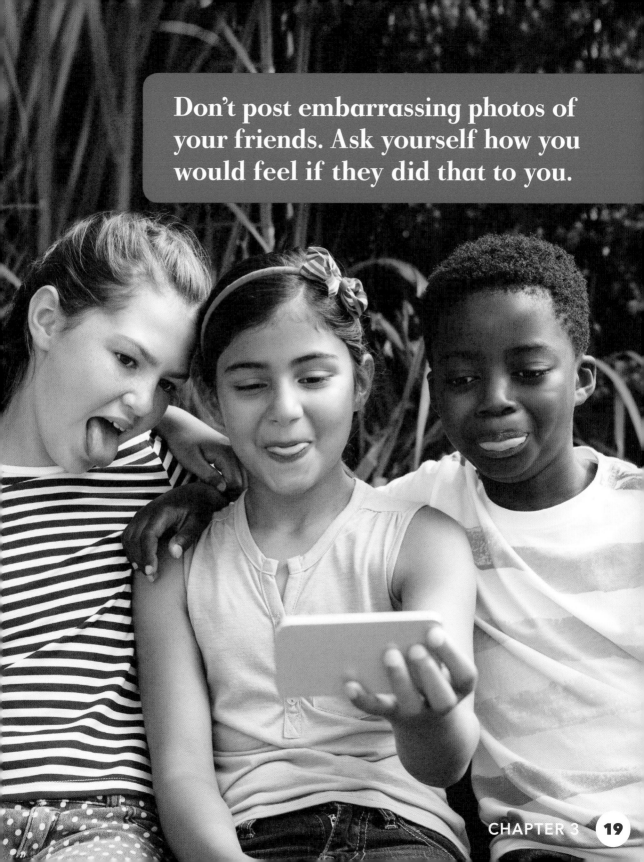

Don't post embarrassing photos of your friends. Ask yourself how you would feel if they did that to you.

If you see something online that disturbs you, shut it off. Don't show it to your friends. Report it to an adult.

It might feel like the things you do online don't matter in real life. But everything that happens online can affect someone. Including you! Make sure your actions are good.

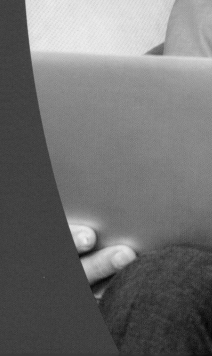

## WHAT DO YOU THINK?

As you get older, you may apply for jobs. Make new friends. Go to college. People may look to see what you have done online. Are you leaving a positive **digital footprint**?

# ACTIVITIES & TOOLS

## STAY SAFE ONLINE

Follow these steps to stay safe online.

1. Ask an adult before creating accounts on social media and websites. Create usernames that don't include your real name.

2. Ask an adult before downloading applications or software. Make sure they are from a trusted source.

3. Create unique passwords for your accounts.

4. Check the privacy settings of your accounts and use them.

5. Never give out your age, full name, phone number, address, or school name.

6. Never give information about your family members, including their addresses, names, and where they work or go to school.

7. Never send photos to strangers.

**cyberbullies:** People who post or do harmful things to others online.

**digital footprint:** The information about a particular person that exists on the Internet as a result of online activity.

**malware:** Software that is intended to harm or create problems.

**personal information:** Information, such as one's birth date, address, Social Security number, email address, phone number, or bank account number, that can be used to identify, contact, or locate someone.

**phishing:** The activity of trying to steal someone's identity or information by lying.

**pop-up windows:** Windows that suddenly appear on your computer screen.

**privacy:** The state of being free from being observed or disturbed by other people.

**social media:** Forms of electronic communication through which users create and share information.

**Social Security number:** A number assigned by the government to track social security benefits and for identification.

**software:** Computer programs that control the workings of the equipment, or hardware, and direct it to do specific tasks.

**viruses:** Computer programs that are disguised as a program or file and that can produce copies of itself and insert them in programs to damage or steal information.

## INDEX

## TO LEARN MORE

**Finding more information is as easy as 1, 2, 3.**

1. Go to www.factsurfer.com
2. Enter "stayingsafeonline" into the search box.
3. Click the "Surf" button to see a list of websites.

**FACT SURFER**